TIM
LEE

Contents

You just can't play a depressing song
on the banjo.

—STEVE MARTIN[1]

Tim Lee

Let's Get Small,
Steve Martin, 1977

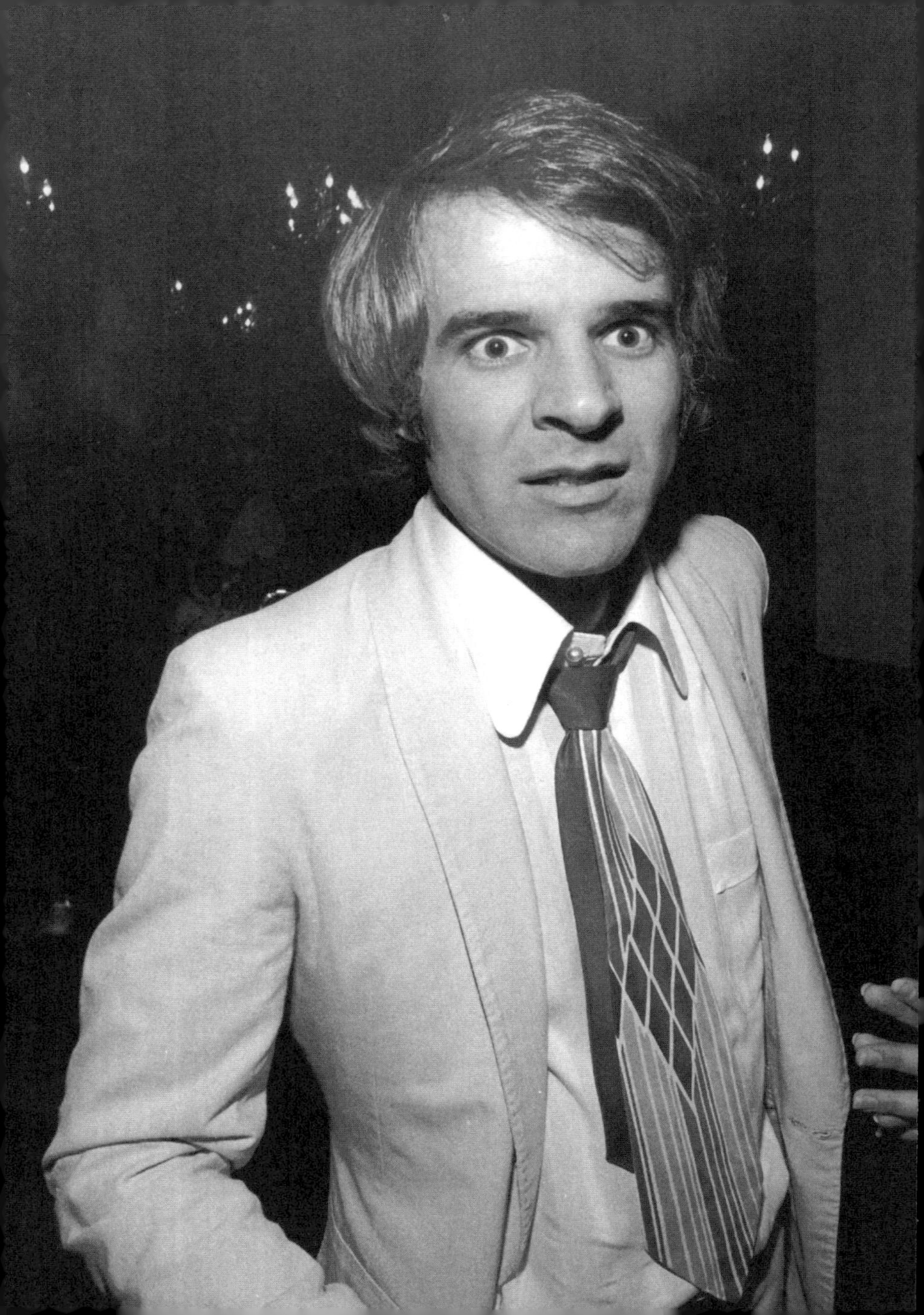

… And so it goes: What happens when an individual becomes entangled in his own freedom? In 1977 Steve Martin recorded *Let's Get Small* at the Boarding House in San Francisco. A rambling, formless, swirling comedy album, it played the steady conventions of the standard live stand-up routine against the ever-increasing absurdity of a comedian who seemed incapable of telling a straight joke. Incomprehension, mad panic, and a deadpan intensity are strategies Martin used to test and upend the conventional limits of the modern comedian, and, like any good (ir)rational artist, Martin acknowledged the normalizing effects of a stable structure only by his desire and ambition to knock it down. Most of his stand-up work internalizes this punklike attitude to a degree; if he's aggressive in his relationship with the audience, it is only because he badly wants them to understand. With stark informality, he essentially works to fracture and upset the codes of "normal" social behavior —through abrupt, rhetorical speech, bold-faced egocentrism, and a godlike claim to omniscience— in order to posit strange new ways of apprehending them. And in *Let's Get Small*, he accomplishes no less than to effectively reveal the large extent to which comedy can deify antisocial behavior by creating an unhinged spectacle of ridiculous activity. In other words, here is the abnormal as a new, formalized norm. And as Martin devoted his early comedy to investigating the arbitrary and the disproportionate, it was his self-imposed amnesty from behavioral standards that allowed him the liberty to act wildly. In his mind, articulating various new attempts at humor became commensurate with a type of social freedom. Yet as he pursued his interest in rewriting the terms of stand-up while relativizing behavioral conventions in delirious ways, the basic question behind this random performativity was: Toward what purpose? As Martin once stated:

> *The crucial thing in performing is to find a choice that works for a moment and isn't the choice anyone else would have made. It's a discipline: You can't just do anything, but you can't do what's expected, either.*[2]

Indeed, if movements and schools are specialized, familiar typologies by which American comedic history is traditionally told—beginning with the minstrel show, leading to vaudeville, leading to Borscht Belt, leading to screwball, leading to nightclub, leading to topical humor, leading to postmodern irony, and so on—this must have rankled Martin, who, in his fugitive thinking, might have considered this ongoing trajectory and thought better to work his way sideways from it.[3] Nonetheless, a central paradox remains. If jokes, by their own definitive nature, thrive off the unwieldy and unexpected, then a good gag should never arrive unsurprisingly. This logic can be confounding only if taken too literally (which, of course, Martin does). If comedy—in its pure, ungainly forms and sparse, erratic reasoning—chaotically advances via its own unpredictability, then, paradoxically, the expectation is that good humor should never come across in ways that can be anticipated.

Playing unpredictability against a structure that thrives off that same uncertainty seems a too-perfect anachronism. And yet here was Martin's stand-up act as a potential radical stratagem, a deliriously accelerating pantomime of jokes-within-a-joke—

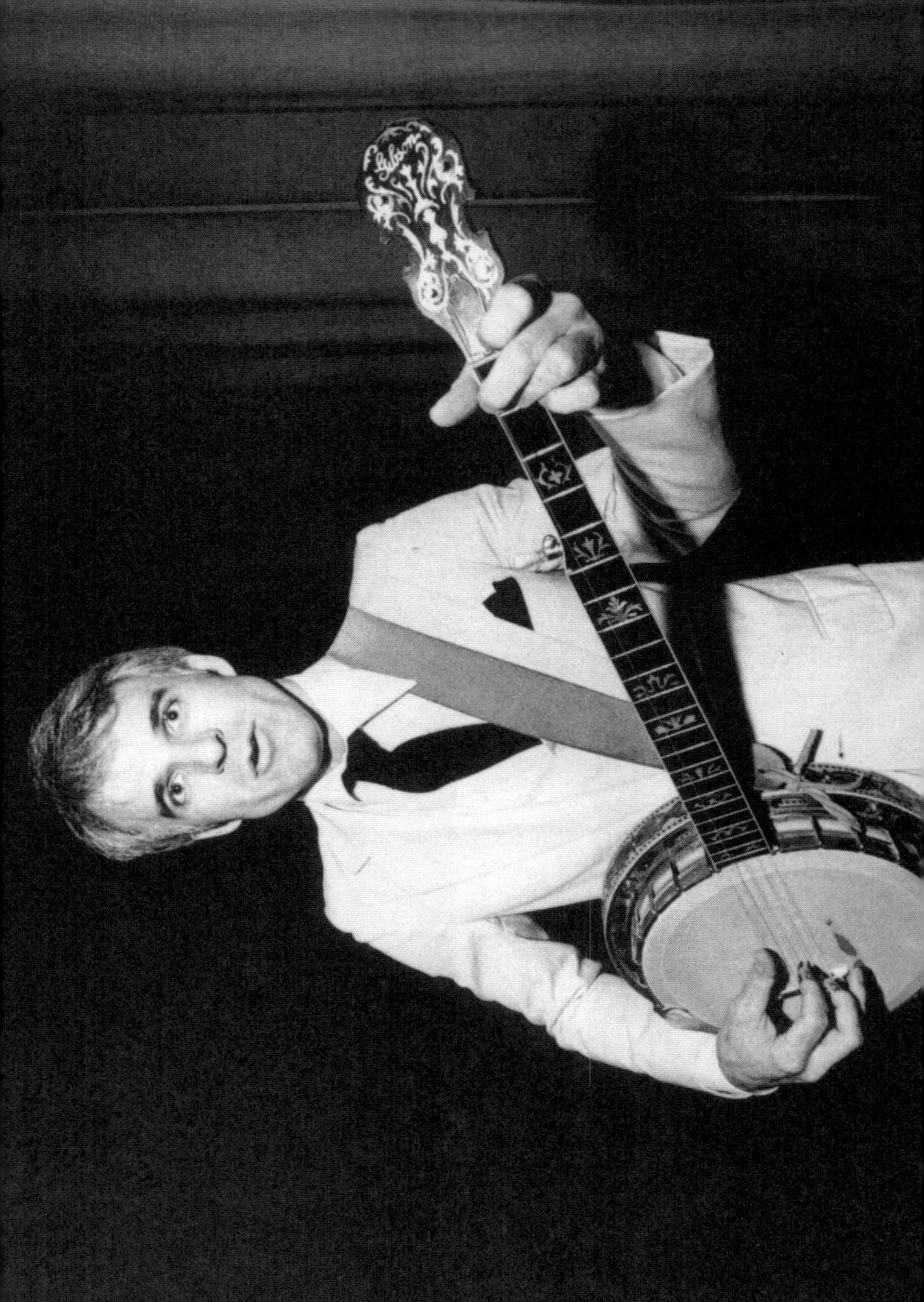

arrows through the head, random musical interludes, brash insults, non sequiturs, and inexplicable gestures—aligned side by side like a series of infinitely regressing tropes. Therein lay the compounding irony. With an act meant not so much to produce laughs as to provoke disarray and confusion (which, in itself, is humorous) the problem that Martin seemed to essentialize was how to react against this expectation of the unexpected in an unpredictable way. For Martin, this dilemma—the implacable divide between comedic norms and the unpredictable upending of unpredictability—provided the vexed thinking toward finding the perfect loophole. Is it possible, for instance, for a comedian to invert his relationship with the crowd, and have his audience entertain *him?* That acute compulsion to rewrite the terms of expectation comes through at the start of *Let's Get Small.* As the shrill twang of the banjo introduces the album, the presumptions for normal comedy are immediately altered; and were it not played with such surprising skill and simple charm, Martin's musicianship would not register as being both expert and sincere. Still, while the built-in tones and echoes of the banjo could be qualified as both wacky and antic, the offbeat disjointedness of the instrument coupled with the bizarre, out-of-context associations (playing bluegrass standards for laughs) provide Martin with an oddly perfect conduit for his modern anticomedy. From its inception, the unpredictable allure of the scenario is immediately disarming. As the audience enjoys Martin's musical playing, their conventional comedic expectations recede, leaving instead the beguiling vision of a white-haired white man in a white suit playing a white four-and-a-half-string guitar.

The high theatricality of the getup—an overexaggerated disguise that amplified Martin's Waspish looks with a blanket, monochrome all-overness—was key, simply because the very image of the autonomous white male, which normally is sustained by a stable regularity, came across instead as uneven and perplexing. When Martin played against his straight-man appearance by acting out abnormal routines, the spasmodic actions and eruptions of wildness were recognizable as peculiar partly because the very conception of a white man's panic is both uncommon and irregular. Therein lies a knowingness, hysterically instilled by Martin in articulating his own mystified state and the strange, uncanny ways in which the backward pathology of his comedy unambiguously provoked a heightened consciousness toward the political unconscious of his comic persona. That is to say, if the recognition of these terms—artistic experimentation, social freedom, and the vacancy of an ascendant individual—is what made Martin's act inherently political, it was because the spectacle of a figure of authority gone unhinged resonated as a crisis not only of power but also of the norms that sustained it. All of which leads to the question: Whose norms? If a by-product of Martin's stand-up was the problematization of normal behavior, *Let's Get Small* did a lot to demonstrate a backward theorem by upending not just the myriad categories of social convention, but also the critical disclosure of how an impure and libidinous freedom might uncover how backward those norms really are.

This is, by compos mentis thinking, a bewildering accomplishment. The grand achievement of Martin's

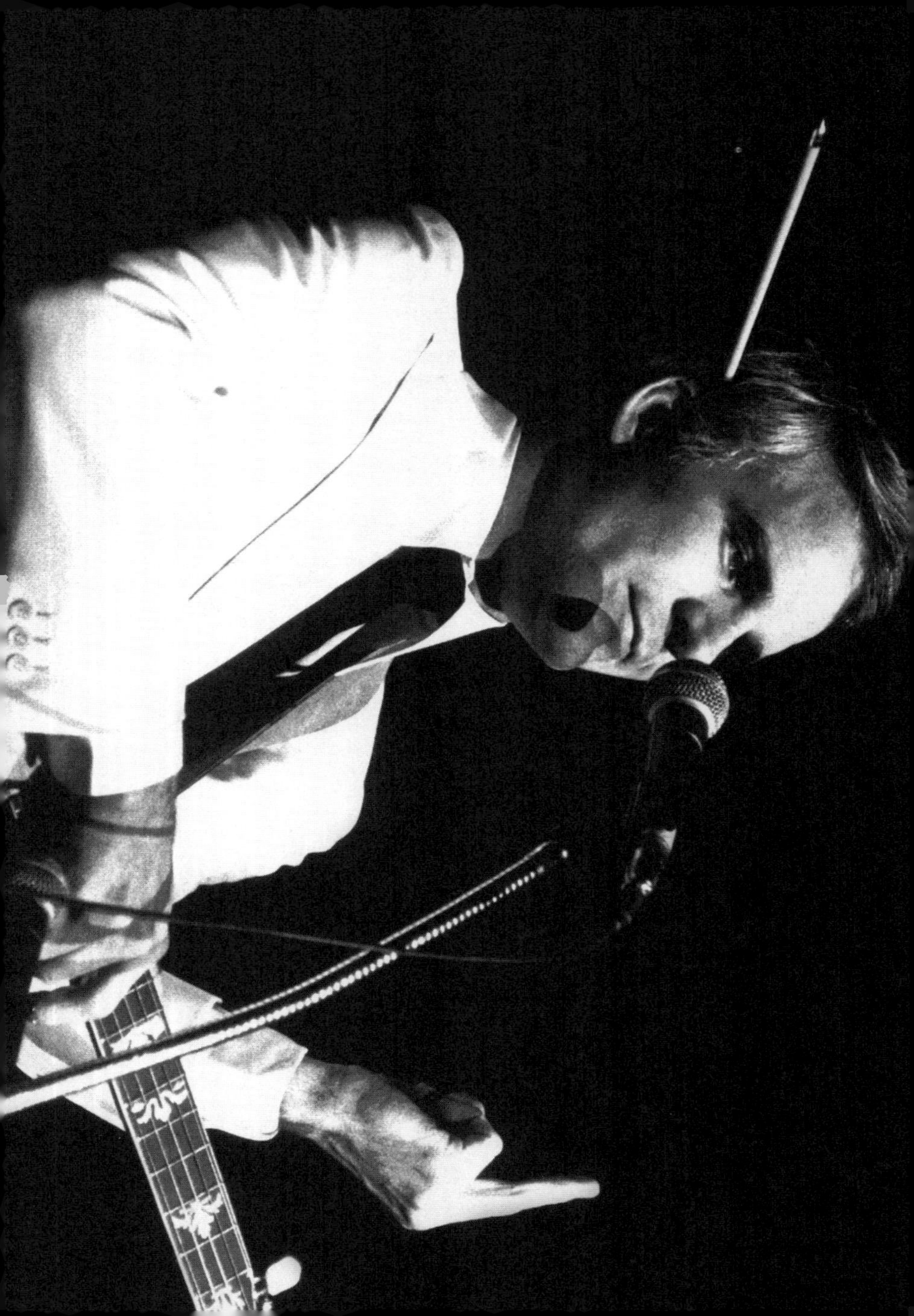

comedy was that it destabilized the field it arrived into while making that instability just one of many topics. And yet, what if that recklessness—so important to a philosophy of unpredictability—attained its own level of expectation and convention? Perhaps inevitably, the very model of artistic liberty that Martin worked to inscribe would soon become a strategy that would hold him captive, the resultant danger being that once the audience got in on the joke, the real humor would be lost, and expecting the unexpected would become the new way of apprehending things.

Nonetheless, if Martin gave up his stand-up act because of this awkward triumphalism, his turn toward a newfound austerity signaled the status of someone wanting to be taken seriously. The restraint in his later performances—conditioned by a knowledge of his early hysteria—may have been either the result of an inward decision to move on, or, more covertly, another twist on convention. By searching for a freedom from freedom, the continuing irony may be that Martin's emancipation from comedy was unexpectedly located on a more dramatically conservative course. Perhaps to sometimes get something right is to purposefully do it wrong, and for Martin this is a form of disavowal toward which he continues to exhibit a random philosophy that has the potential to perpetuate on its own: freely, continually, persistently, endlessly . . .

1. Dialogue from Steve Martin's *Let's Get Small* (Warner Bros., 1977).

2. Adam Gopnik, "Steve Martin: The Late Period," *The New Yorker*, November 29, 1993, 98.

3. Dialogue from *Let's Get Small*: "I don't know what you heard about my show, you probably heard I was into the comedy thing. But I kinda want to get out of that now and get more into the music."

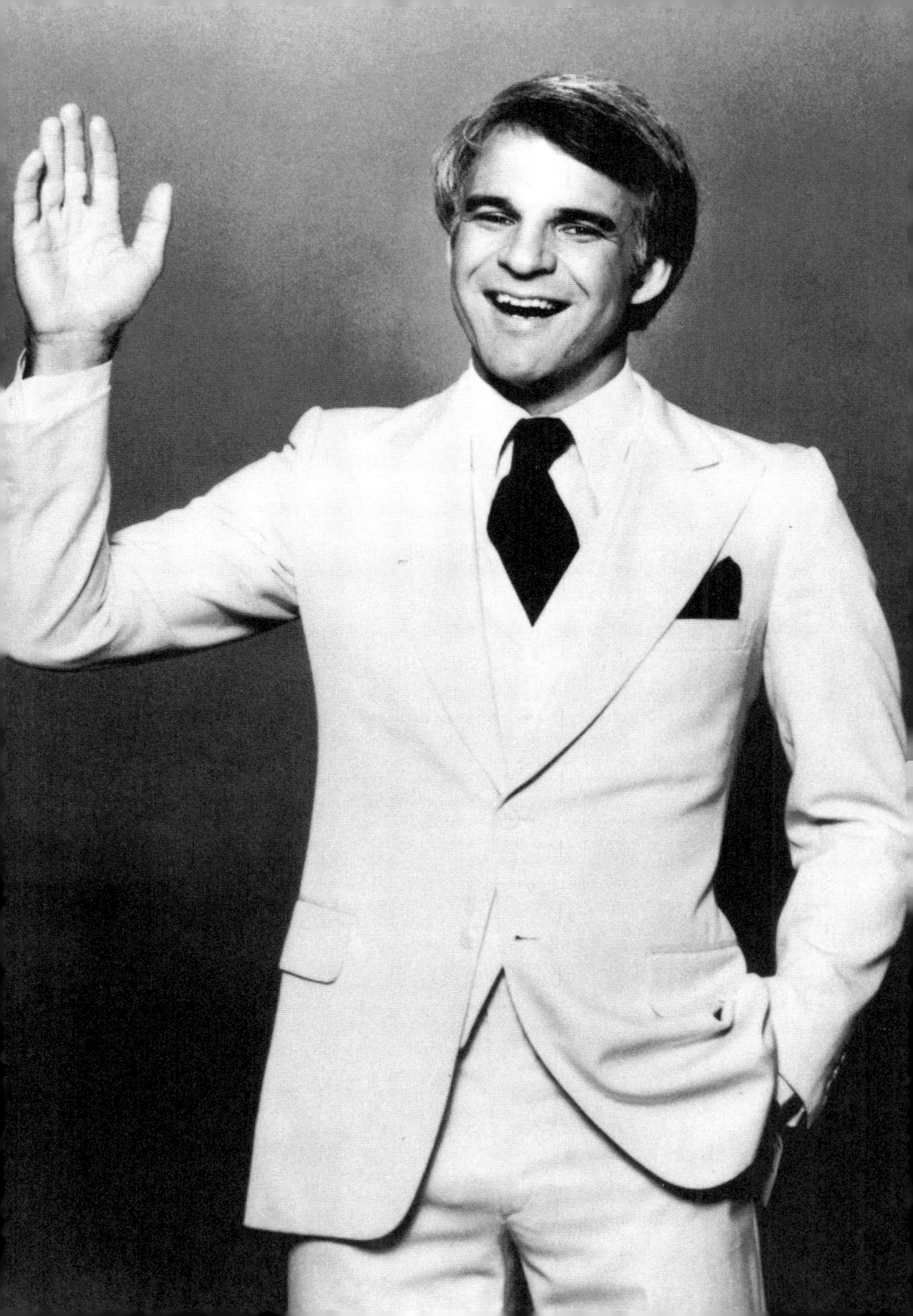

Heart of Gold *put me in the middle of the road. Traveling there soon became a bore so I headed for the ditch.*

—NEIL YOUNG[1]

Tim Lee

Rust Never Sleeps, Neil Young, 1979

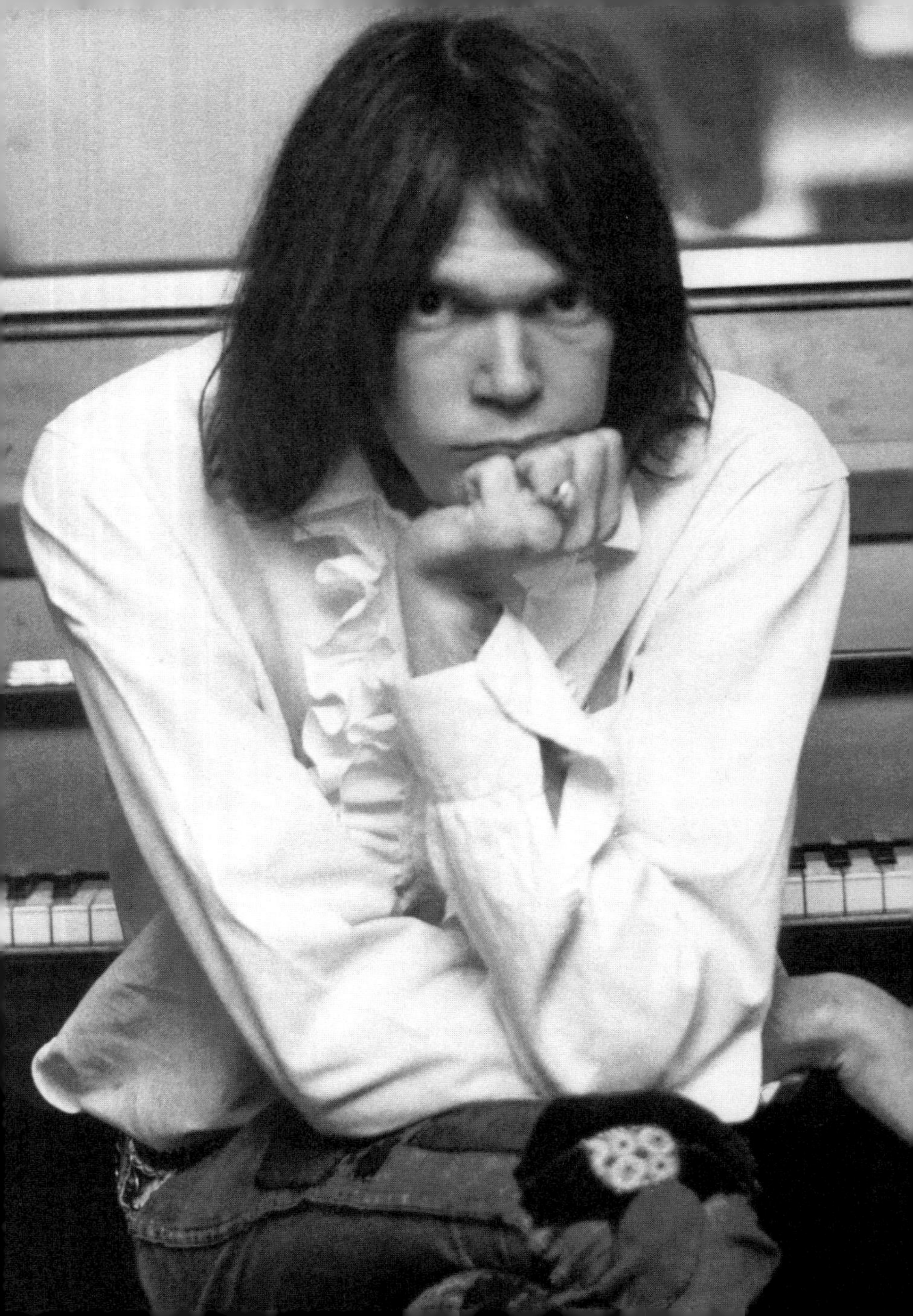

… Restless, dissonant, singular, circular? In 1979 Neil Young released *Rust Never Sleeps*, which he recorded live at the Cow Palace in San Francisco. A compound concert/concept album divided into two distinct parts, the first half acoustic, the second half electric, the record is both urgent and mythic, mournful yet unrepentant, passive and aggressive. This doubleness typifies the contradictory multitudes of the album. While the back-and-forth between the two sides encompasses many opposites—bridging, for instance, the twin sensations of stillness and noise, contrasting moods of sorrow and revolt, and the historical divide between folk and rock—the resultant totality effects a strange dissonance. Altogether schizoid and whole, and interpretable not so much as a rift between extremes as a composite mishmash of disparate codes, *Rust Never Sleeps* comes off as a bold, even unstable, creation.

That instability, of course, is full of purpose and comes with motivations that are volatile in themselves. Throughout his career Young has always played the restless agitator of rock music, a tradition that he actively helped inscribe, up against the edifying upheavals of experimentation, of which *Rust Never Sleeps* is an exemplary example. With expressions that veer from the somber and melancholic to the aggressive and insistent, the album's conceptual middle is illuminated by its first and last songs. Performed acoustically (first) and electrically (second), and with a starkness of difference that connotes competing associations, "My My, Hey Hey (Out of the Blue)" and "Hey Hey, My My (Into the Black)" provide formal bookends to the record, expressive in their respective genres, while producing variegated responses to the album's central thematic: the double bind of artistic progress.

For, indeed, emanating from a late-1970s moment defined by the antagonisms brought forth by punk rock, "My My, Hey Hey (Out of the Blue)" and "Hey Hey, My My (Into the Black)" are simultaneously expressive of the master narrative of continuous progress through the interpretive split that divides the former's elegy of the past from the latter's edict for the future. With differences between the two songs marked not

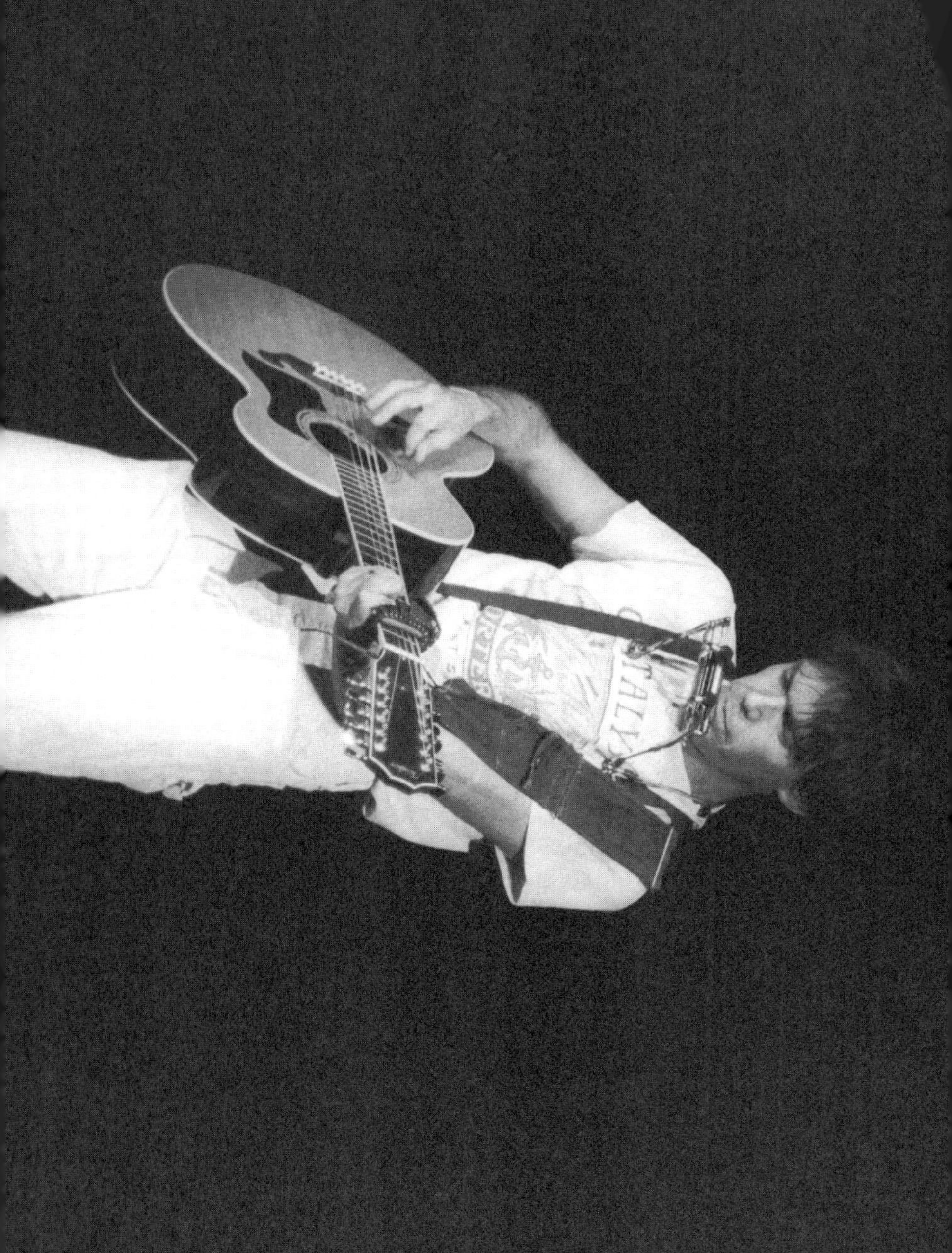

only by polarities in volume but also by nuances in
language, the grammatical flip that alternates the
outwardly attentive call of "Hey Hey" with the inward
utterance of "My My" might distinguish the acoustic
"My My, Hey Hey . . ." as the introspective voice of
an aging folk singer reflecting on the past, while the
electric "Hey Hey, My My . . ." could be unscrambled
as the youthful punk rocker making a declaration for
the ever-changing future. As Young sings, "The king
is gone but he's not forgotten." Generations recede,
music changes, paradigms shift. And with the process
presented as not so much unchanging but inevitable,
both versions present these transformations not only
as artistically ongoing and historically inexorable,
but also as individually afflicting and vexatious.

Rust Never Sleeps plays off this binary consciousness.
Through warped-mirror images of the same song,
the record acts as a signifier for the restlessness and
never-ending agitation that has characterized much
of Young's career. From folk to psychedelia, swing to
garage, electronic to country, he has pitched a refusal
to stand still directly to the sensations of newness,

with their modern alienations and old narratives.
And if each album destabilizes the one that came
before it while setting the stage for its own inevitable
upending, it is because this sprawling unpredictability permeates much of Young's life: the retro-future
individual both archaic and modern; the rail-thin
American revolutionary from Canada; the edgy teen-
ager from Toronto who drove to California in a hearse;
and now an elder statesman at the Grand Ole Opry. In
1984, as the United States reelected Ronald Reagan, he
bashed the welfare system and vocally supported the
"trigger-happy cowboy"; 20 years later we find him
castigating the new conservative regime and protest-
ing the new war.

And on it goes: If the drift of Young's life suggested a
restlessness about his politics, it also made for a stag-
geringly vital art. His free movement among genres,
coupled with his continued, accelerated production,
signaled a type of formlessness that, while amorphous
and in flux, nonetheless became identifiable—the
indefinite made distinct. And after four decades
of reacting against his own reactions, the pattern of

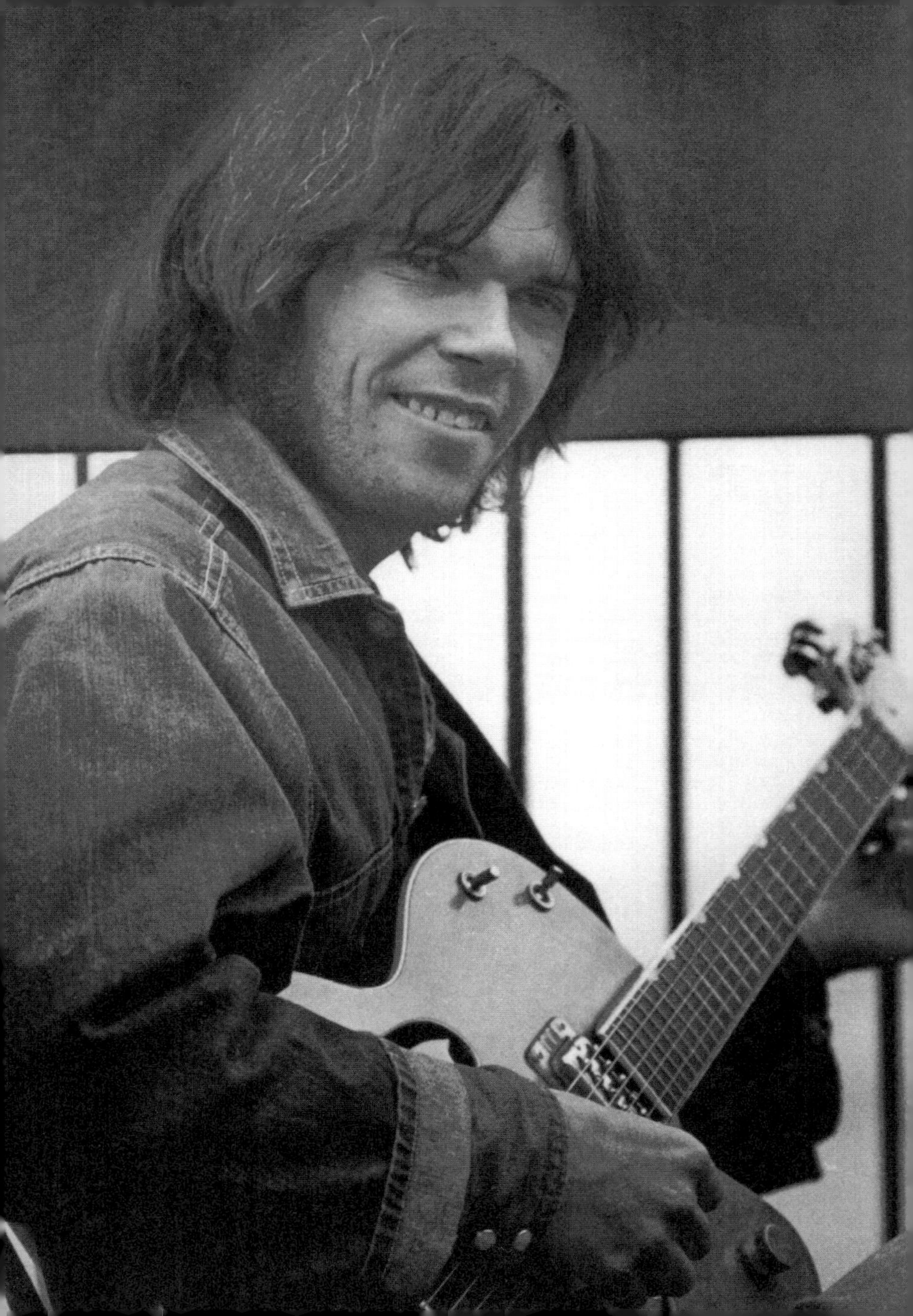

Young's life asserts itself as a sort of messy design marked by intervals of anxious rejuvenation: "If I play the same kind of music for too long, I lose it. And I have to stop playing that kind of music until I've got the feeling back."[2]

Young's work often exhibits this self-consciousness. Indeed, there are few things of which one could be more self-conscious than being self-obsessed with looking at how one looks at things. This is the very question of subjectivity, and Young's wayward take on the world is an offbeat panopticon that assumes a multitude of potential positions. Thus the seeming indecision, the ongoing contradictions, and the easy shifts that allow him to play the rogue stylist.

These styles are, of course, many, and altogether idiosyncratic. In this regard, Young is singular in conveying the sense that patterns should not so much take hold as constantly change, and his faith in this unruly ethos assumes an intensity that is no less mystifying in its generative totality than comprehensible as a motivation for endless progress. Yet it is the very subject of progress that makes *Rust Never Sleeps* so artfully compelling, in that the album showcases how the impetus for artistic advancement—particularly when engaged self-consciously—was psychologically destabilizing while it established instability as a persistent narrative of Young's career.

This process is certainly strange, partly because it is imbued with a certain restlessness that, however dissonant, can never remain completely incongruous so long as the upheavals participate in asserting an overall pattern. Moving from *Neil Young* to *Chrome Dreams II*, and from 1968 to the present, if all of Young's progressive breaks and reactions take on the form of a sequential line, then that line—growing more convoluted through the passing years—eventually becomes a complete circle. Thus the arc of Young's history, however unpredictable, can be characterized as a series of myriad digressions, with each album destabilizing the preceding one, and the ongoing succession of these responses leading to an inevitable return to where he began.

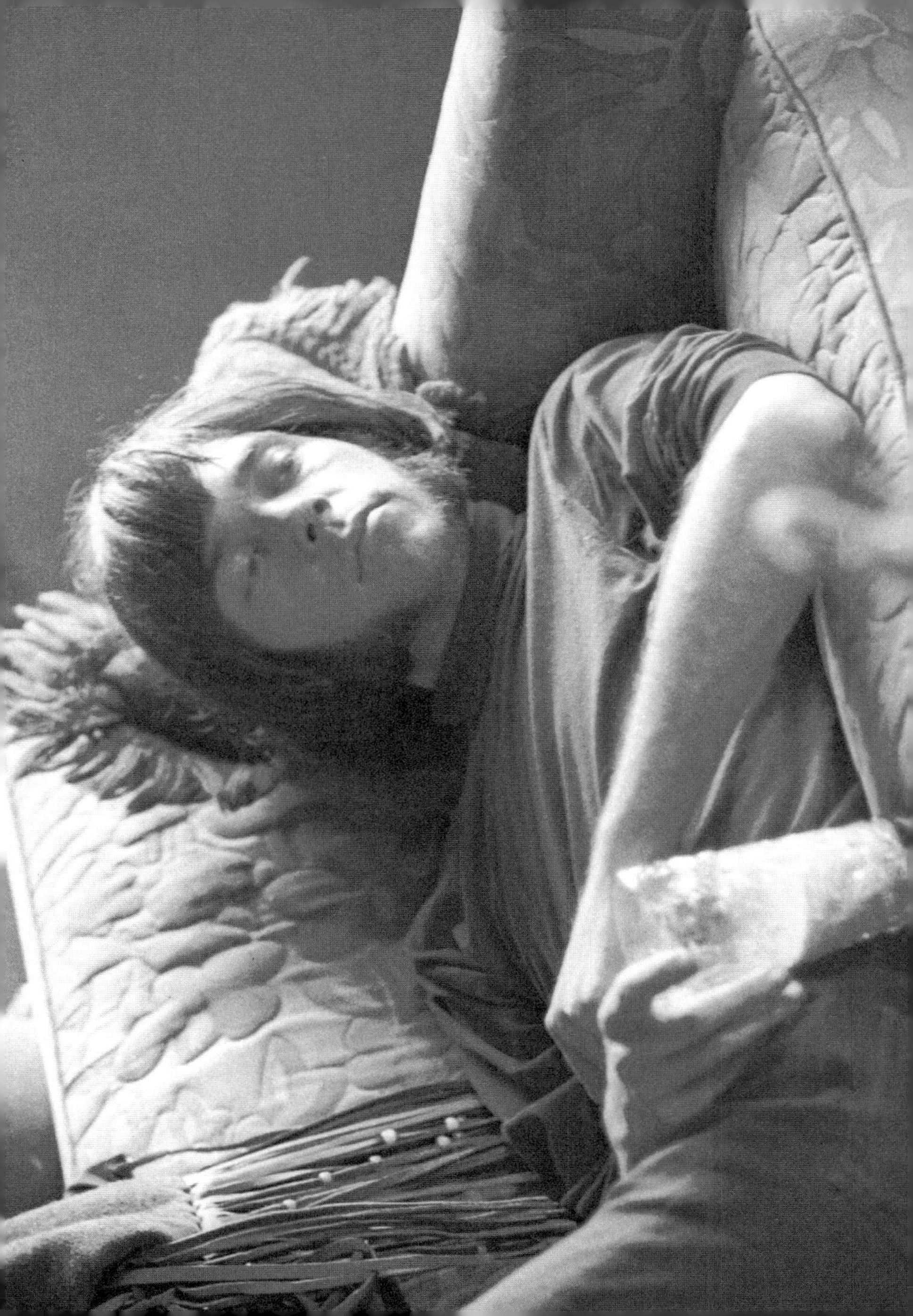

The circularity of this process is telling, for it suggests that an artist, in his search for newness, might actually find himself rearticulating an initial concern. *Rust Never Sleeps* reflects this thinking; in contradictory ways, the experimental structure of the album animates these traditional notions of creative origins through its struggle for innovation. Or, rather, is it about the struggle among these forces and the persistence of that struggle as a frozen conflict? The perpetuity of this narrative—and of this conflict at a standstill—may sustain itself simply because it is not so much persistent as inescapable. And yet the very permanence of the conflict is revealing, since it effects an odd thinking toward artistic autonomy in a way that is commensurate with perpetual change and instability. If Young's restlessness creates a dissonance that articulates his own individuality, the circuitous route of his experimentations can only reinforce his own self-consciousness, doubling over itself by folding inward and circulating within, constantly reacting, forever regressing, becoming multitudes . . .

1. From the liner notes for the album *Decade* (Reprise Records, 1977).

2. As quoted in Karen Schoemer's "At the Deli with Neil Young: Still Searching For a Heart of Gold," *The New York Times*, November 25, 1992.

Jens Hoffmann

The Art
of Laughter

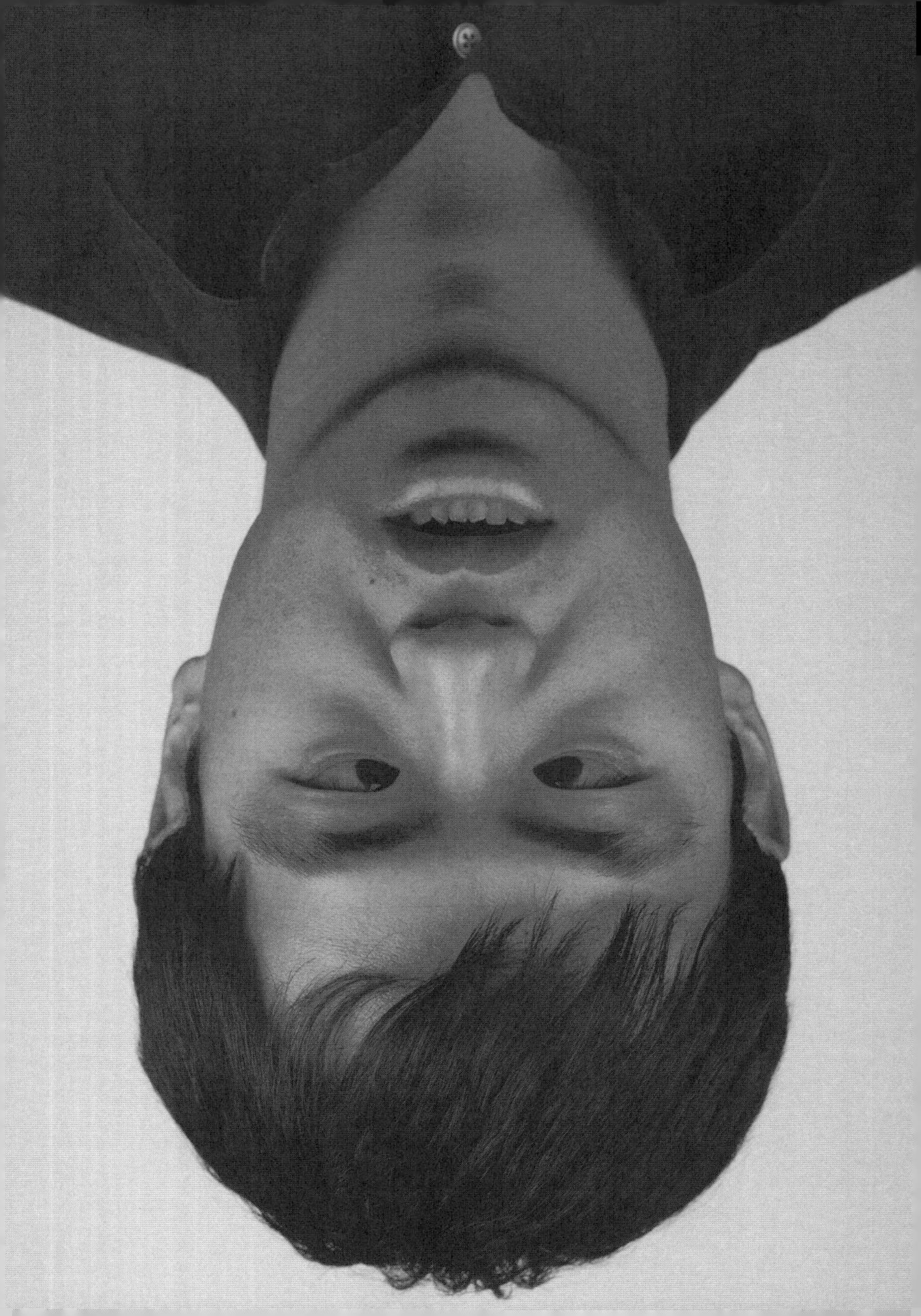

Art and humor are both exclusively human terrain. No tree can tell a joke, and no horse or chicken can make a painting.

To say that some artists are comedians and some comedians are artists is not controversial. But what exactly does an artist have in common with a comedian? For a start, they both need an audience—

The Jerk, Carl Reiner, 1979, 2004 Chromogenic print 84 x 72 in. (213.4 x 182.9 cm)

listeners capable of understanding the circumstances that make a joke funny, or viewers capable of appreciating the context in which a work of art expresses meaning. Artists and comedians have to play with, and within, culturally accepted rituals and structures to bring their creations to fruition. Their success depends on their ability to address their audiences through strategies that lead to recognition without giving away the subject of the joke or artwork too soon. A comedian entertains people by making them laugh, and an artist engages viewers by making them reflect. And, ideally, they should be able to trade roles: A comedian should provoke us to contemplate and an artist should entertain us. Both, in their best work, challenge the way we view the world, point to complex issues, offer relief from the pressures of the everyday, and

create meaning by resolving ten-
sions, conflicts, and anxieties.

Comedians as well as artists often
draw from their own biographies
(and occasionally induce feelings of
embarrassment when the work is too
personal) yet often manage to find
strength in their own weaknesses
and expose the vulnerability in all
of us. Using oneself as the subject of
fun or as raw material for a work has
always been a very successful avenue
for comedians and artists alike,
since practitioners in both fields are
bound to very particular cultural and
political contexts that are difficult
to transcend. What might be funny

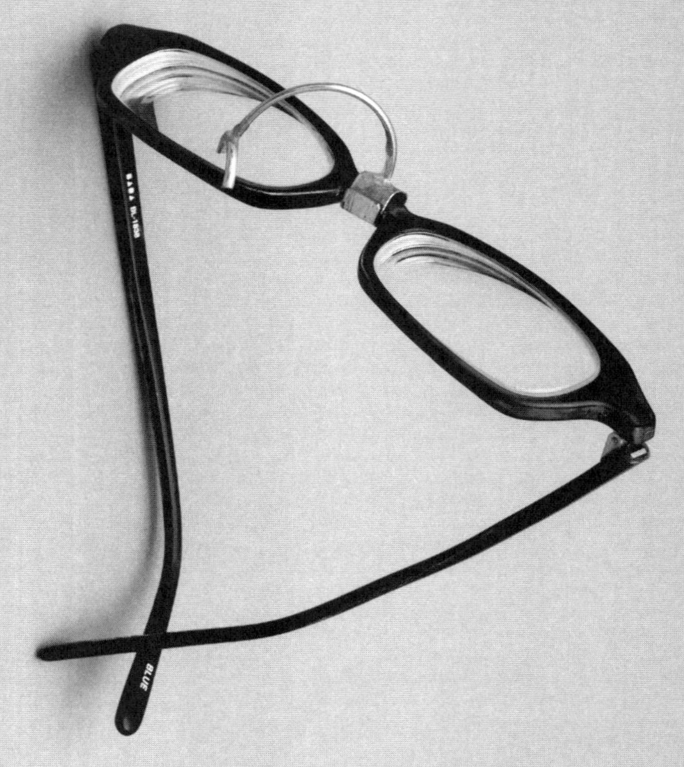

in America might not get a laugh
in Asia, and what a European artist
does might not interest anyone in
Africa. The appreciation of a work
is always subjective and a matter of
personal and cultural taste.

At their most powerful, artists
and comedians are rebellious
and insubordinate, effecting
change by questioning authori-
ties and hierarchies. Their position
in society allows them to express
what their audiences may not even
dare to think, revealing sensitive
truths about the culture and its
worries, hurts, and fears. They can
violate social conventions and

taboos, or make us look differently at the trivial and the ordinary. In this sense, many comedians are, in fact, artists. Who would deny that label to Buster Keaton, Harold Lloyd, or the Marx Brothers, given the elaborate degree of sophistication they achieved within the genre?

And what about artists as comedians? One might think, dismissively, that it is quite a distance from the peaks of high art to the lows of one-liners, puns, and sideshow gags. Yet the many connections between art and comedy are undeniable, and the role of humor in contemporary art has been the focus of several recent art-historical and curatorial explorations. Many of these have focused on the subversive, analyzing how artists have appropriated humor and comedy to tell jokes and be funny in a way that undermines the ostensibly serious field of visual art.

The origins of the phenomenon trace back quite a ways. William Hogarth, working in the early eighteenth century, made critical and satirical paintings that depicted with humor the social hardships and political misfortunes of his time. And so did several painters of the early Renaissance, for instance Lucas Cranach, who combined religious pathos and philosophical humor to strong effect, and Hieronymus Bosch, whose apocalyptic paintings incorporated a strong dose of dark humor. Michelangelo was known during his life for his great sense of humor, though today the serious character of his work is what is best remembered. And Pieter Bruegel's paintings are renowned for their depictions of the humor, horror, and beauty of a time when levity was necessary for survival.

After the relatively sober eighteenth and nineteenth centuries, during which humor was perceived as a lower genre, not serious enough for the ambitions of high art, the modern era has without a doubt witnessed a significant resurgence of the trend. Comedy's antiauthoritarian applications proved attractive and useful to the Dadaists, for instance Kurt Schwitters with *Ursonate* (1922) and Marcel Duchamp with his somewhat cynical readymades. And since the rebellious 1960s, concepts of parody, irony, and the absurd have become ever more prevalent, as in the work of Piero Manzoni, Andy Warhol, John Baldessari, Richard Hamilton, Sigmar Polke, Martin Kippenberger, and Martha Rosler, to mention only a few.

The idea of a joke does not at first seem particularly complicated. Someone tells a funny story, and others laugh. It is often difficult to say precisely, however, what it is that amuses us and why. Behind this peculiar aspect of human experience lies a complicated cultural mechanism. What one person considers funny might not make another laugh at all. A joke can be elevating and at the same time very upsetting. It can be universal or comprehensible only to a very narrow group. A joke can make friends, and it can make enemies. As a result, humor has fascinated not only artists but also philosophers; it was Ludwig

Wittgenstein who said that a serious piece of philosophy could consist entirely of jokes. From Aristotle to Diogenes, Søren Kierkegaard to Arthur Schopenhauer, Sigmund Freud to Bertrand Russell, sophists through the ages have tried to understand what makes us laugh by examining the logic and metaphysics of humor. While some of these figures apparently had a great sense of humor, they have not always made comedy a laughing matter. One might accuse the French philosopher Henri Bergson of analyzing it to death in "Laughter: An Essay on the Meaning of the Comic" (1911), perhaps the most serious and humorless essay ever written about funny stuff, though it does offer great insights into the comic dimensions of the human mind.

The thought of being serious about being funny brings us to Tim Lee. Lee considers himself someone who takes being funny very seriously. Or, alternatively, someone who makes seriousness fun. Though he calls himself (with some irony) a performance artist, his works most often take the form of photographs and videos, which lately have branched out to involve objects and sculpture. He focuses a critical lens on society, staging complex collisions among iconic artworks, classic Conceptual artists (for instance Dan Graham, Bruce Nauman, and Robert Smithson), canonical moments of popular culture (mostly related to comedy, sports, and music), and issues of racial identity, all within the larger framework of modern history. Lee's works always feature the artist himself, taking ridiculous postures or making absurd gestures in an attempt to create an intentional and highly choreographed travesty of his sources.

Only a few of Lee's works specifically address comedy and humor, yet all of them have comical aspects.

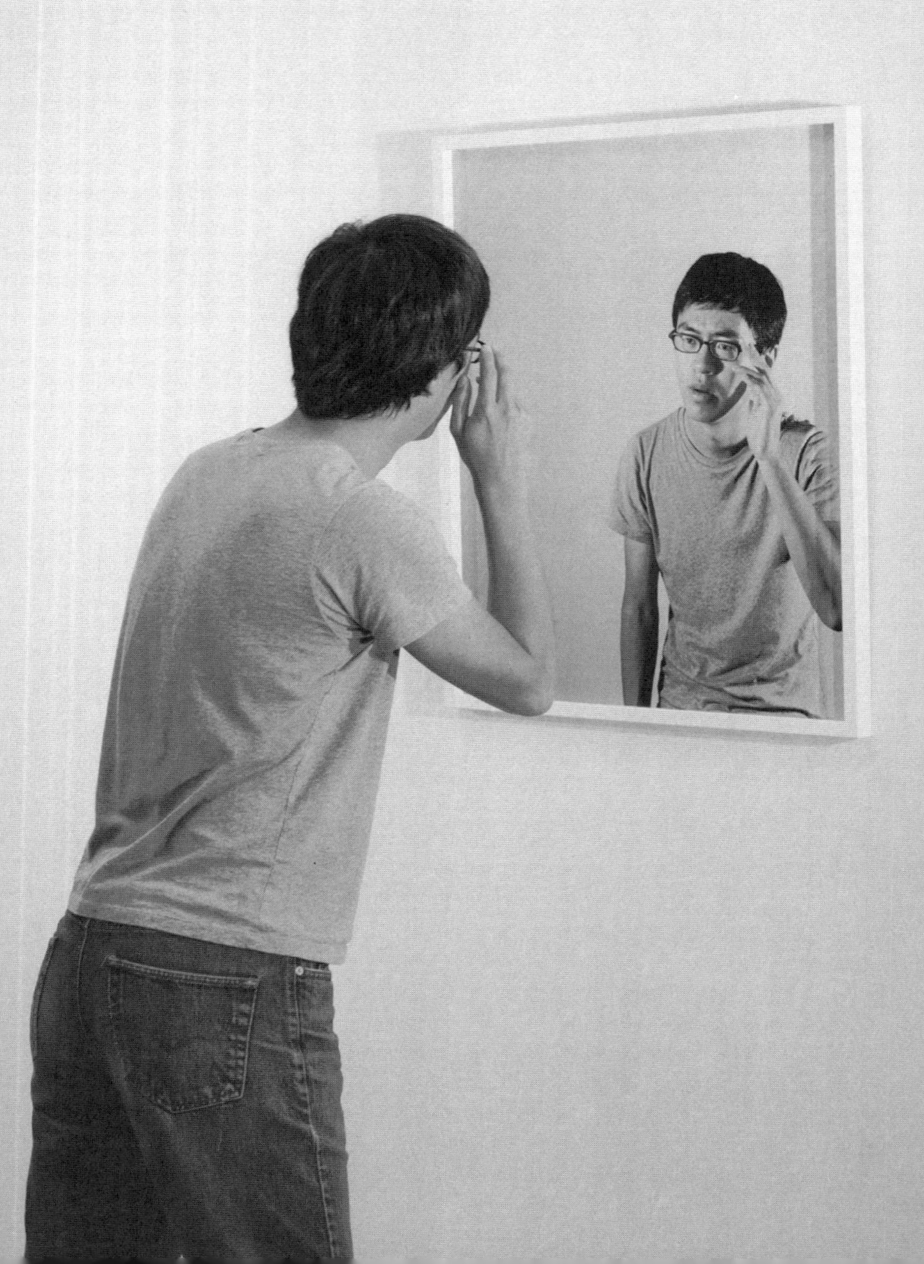

They have a very minimal, clean aesthetic but are full of often-confusing references, layers of dialogue, loopholes, and subnarratives. In one of his earliest pieces, *Duck Soup, The Marx Brothers, 1933* (2002), the artist

conflates Dan Graham's concerns with respect to optical phenomena and behaviorism as presented in one of his most iconic performance pieces, *Performance/Audience/Mirror* (1977) with one of comedy's most famous moments, the mirror scene in the Marx Brothers movie *Duck Soup* (1933). In the photograph we see Lee looking at himself in a mirror, touching his trademark glasses

as if he is not just checking his vision
but in fact touching his own body.
Perhaps he is looking for something
or someone, or lost in a moment
of self-identification, but ultimately
he seems confused by his own
reflection, suggesting a potential
ontological crisis. Connecting
Graham to the Marx Brothers and
the idea of the double take, Lee re-
casts Graham's piece as, ultimately,
a sight gag—a play with basic perception resulting in the occupation
of an off-balance viewpoint.

Steve Martin is another comedian
who has influenced a number of
Lee's works, including *The Jerk, Carl*

Reiner, 1979 (2004), *Untitled (Steve Martin, 1972)* (2005), and most recently *Untitled (The Pink Panther, 2049)* and *Untitled (The Pink Panther, 2092)* (both 2007). The first of these is probably Lee's most hilarious piece. In a ludicrously large photographic print (seven by six feet), the artist appears cross-eyed and upside down. The work is primarily a reference to Steve Martin's 1979 film *The Jerk*, directed by Carl Reiner. The film is a narrative of self-exploration embedded within the absurd plot of a late-1970s Hollywood comedy. Martin plays Navin Johnson, a man-child searching for his own identity who becomes a millionaire overnight by inventing a ridiculous device called the Opti-Grab (also the subject of another work by Lee). The success of the Opti-Grab is short-lived, as Martin's character is sued by Carl Reiner, playing him-self in the film, who has become cross-eyed from using it. The photograph's formal inversion is a comic com-ment on the narrative of the film, and also a nod to the artist Rodney Graham, who in 1979 (the same year the movie was made) produced the seminal work *Camera Obscura,* introducing the flipped-image tech-nique that would become one of his major artistic strategies. Lee's

Untitled (The Pink Panther, 2092), 2007
Two chromogenic prints
60 x 48 in. (152.4 x 121.9 cm)

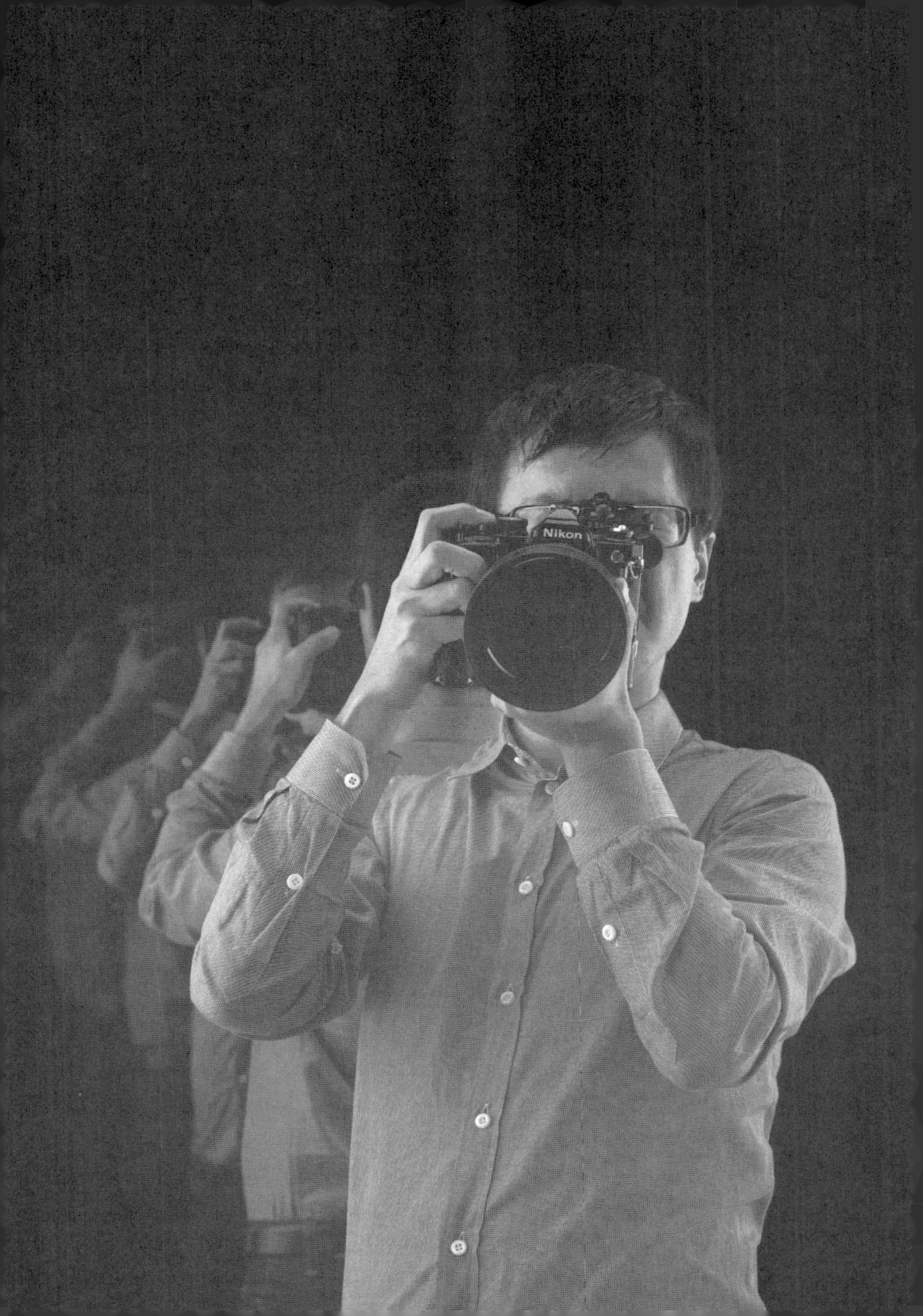

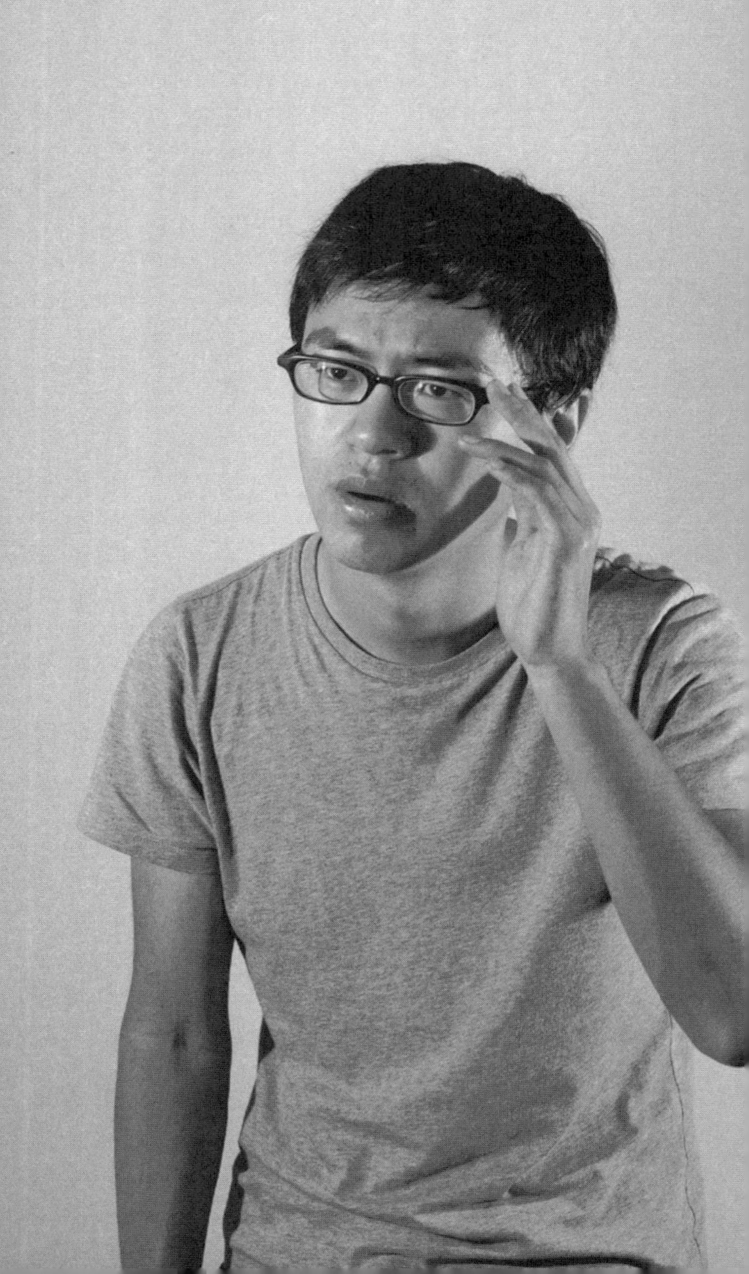

approach creates an analogy between Graham's twists on the conventions of art and Martin's twists on the standards of comedy. And, by paying simultaneous hom-

age to both figures, he sets himself up in a relationship with them that is like the relationship between Martin and Reiner. Lee frequently weaves such complex nets of references and subplots. Invoking Martin, Reiner, Graham, and Lee himself, Lee's picture becomes, in his own words, "a perfect photographic portrait of a perfectly ruined vision."

In *Untitled (Steve Martin, 1972)*, Lee

imagines Martin rehearsing one of his classic poses—playing the banjo with a fake arrow through his head—in front of a mirror. The artist characterizes the piece as a depiction of himself assuming Martin's persona in a hypothetical moment in which Martin was actively constructing *his* persona. Lee views every public figure or celebrity as a deliberate construction, not unlike an artwork. He posed while holding the banjo in his left hand, even though Martin ordinarily holds it in his right. The mirror reflection should have corrected the "mistake," but Lee re-flipped the image in what he calls a triple-stage flip-within-a-flip-within-a-flip, inspired specifically by Dan Graham's interest in playing with perception, and more generally by Graham's and Martin's shared desire to break down the conventions of their respective genres.

Lee invokes the same cast of influential personages in *Untitled (The Pink Panther, 2049)* and *Untitled (The Pink Panther, 2092)*. These works originated in response to the 2006 remake of Blake Edwards's famous comedy *The Pink Panther* (1963), which starred the English actor Peter Sellers as the bumbling French inspector Jacques Clouseau; the remake starred Steve Martin, an

American. Lee's work suggests two new future remakes of the film (in 43-year intervals, just as there were 43 years between the original and the first remake) and conflates all the protagonists' ethnicities, nationalities, and histories into an absurd and confusing narrative of comic misrepresentation. Lee, a Korean Canadian, plays an American who is impersonating an Englishman who is mimicking a Frenchman, thus suggesting that ethnic and national identity, and even subjectivity, are unstable and volatile. He complicates things further by shooting his own image while standing inside one of Dan

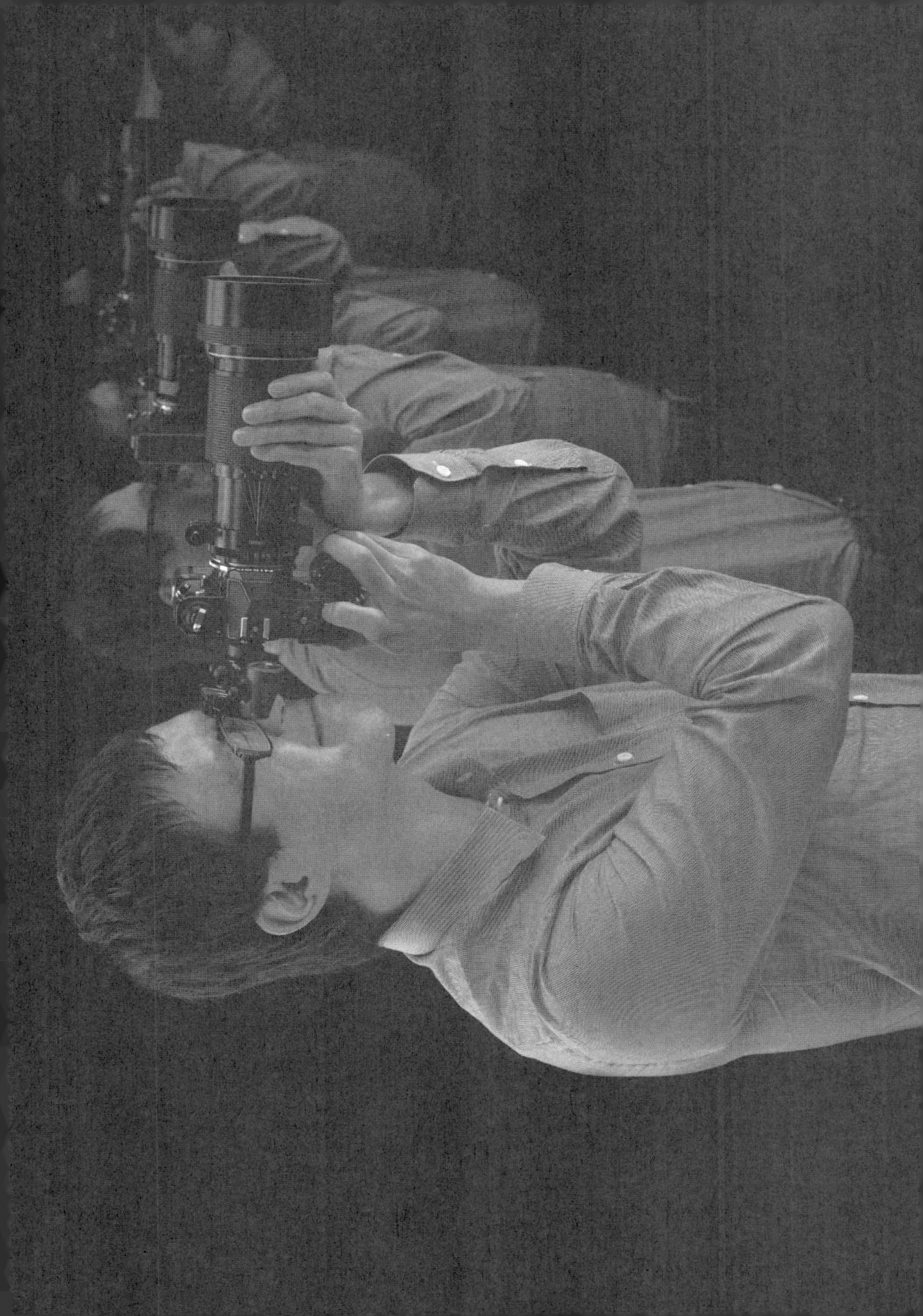

Graham's two-way mirror pavilions using various optical devices such as glasses, cameras, and binoculars. These devices represent the obfuscation, rather than the clarification, of images and perspective, assisting Lee's strategy of taking apart conventional ways of seeing.

Lee's references to humor represent an urge to articulate history, to disrupt artistic traditions and social conventions, and to reveal with subtlety his own social conscience. His use of humor makes the works polemical without ever giving the outward appearance of polemic. Given the number of artists today addressing troubling and complex issues of human existence—political conflicts, social inequality, and the adverse effects of globalization, to name just a few—it is perhaps no surprise that artists and audiences alike might tire of overly earnest approaches, longing instead for more humorous strategies to offer some relief from the horrors. But the most successful of the artists working in this vein do not provide simplistic sanctuaries of escape. Instead they offer a different perspective on the troubling facts of contemporary life and ultimately, hopefully, show the way to resolving some of the antagonisms of our world.

Claire Fitzsimmons

It's Better to Burn Out Than Fade Away

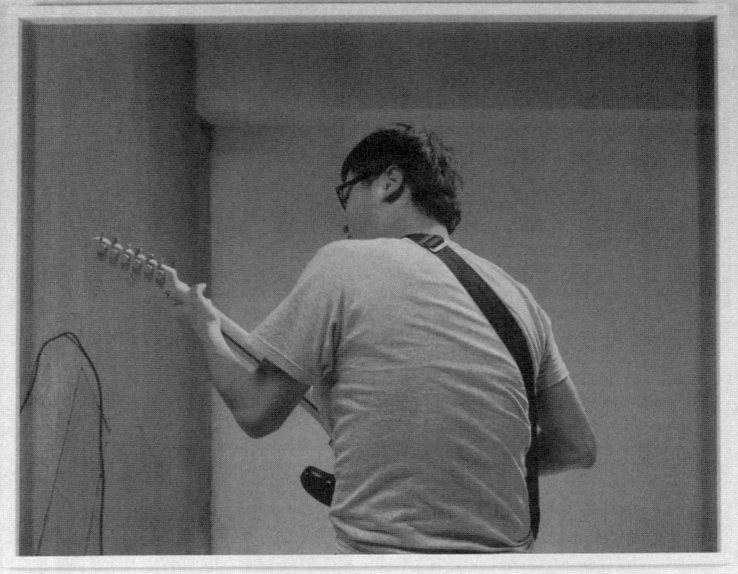
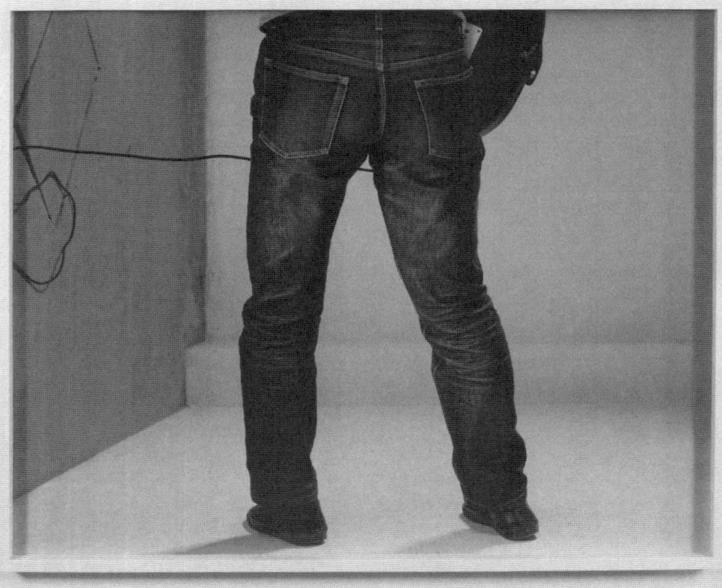

Tim Lee's works have the deceptive appearance of simple self-portraits, but they contain myriad references. Over the last few years the artist has crafted a meticulous persona in his photo- and video-based pieces, which convey, ironically, very little of the personal. Rather, Lee articulates his artistic persona through others trying to articulate theirs. He has assembled something akin to an ensemble cast, drawing his characters—and their accompanying characteristics and ideologies—from an eclectic range of sources. These include major figures of Conceptual art, such as Dan Graham, Robert Smithson, and Bruce Nauman, alongside seminal moments of popular culture, from Carl Reiner's Hollywood movies to Harry Houdini's magic. Since receiving his MFA from the

Untitled (Neil Young, 1968), 2006
Two chromogenic prints
50 ⅞ x 63 in. (129.2 x 160 cm)

University of British Columbia, Vancouver,
in 2002, Lee has created an oeuvre with
a highly theoretical framework, which is
counterbalanced by humor and politics,
in particular issues of race and national
identity.

Capp Street Project is Lee's first artist residency, which is less surprising when one considers that he does not normally work in a site-specific manner (he believes, on the contrary, that all culture travels) and that his usual way of working is a meandering process of reading, research, writing, and production, with the physical artwork realized in a relatively concentrated amount of time. Faced with two clearly defined Capp Street Project parameters—to spend 12 weeks in San Francisco and to deliver a new piece that responds to the local context—Lee had first to work out what, for him, would constitute a residency.

He had his starting point when he discovered that the comedian Steve Martin and the rock musician Neil Young had, coincidentally, both recorded live albums in San Francisco in the late 1970s: *Let's Get Small* at the Boarding House and *Rust Never Sleeps* at the Cow Palace, respectively. Both Martin and Young had appeared, though separately, in several of Lee's previous works, and their postures, props, mannerisms, and language already served as shorthand in his oeuvre for the genres of comedy and rock music.

The residency, then, became an attempt to put Martin and Young together, to create a project that would conflate their different artistic personae and histories while at the same time saying something about culture at large. To solve the dilemma of how to bring these two autonomous figures together, Lee began on paper with a rough diagram

of the arguments for an integrated history. Through writing he gave material form to his attempts to use Martin to understand Young, and vice versa, and his text appears in its final form as the two essays in this publication.

The banjo was among the vital connections Lee uncovered in his research. Young has played the banjo on several recordings, and Martin used the instrument as a prop in his early stand-up routines, including the performance captured on *Let's Get Small*. Martin is actually quite accomplished on the

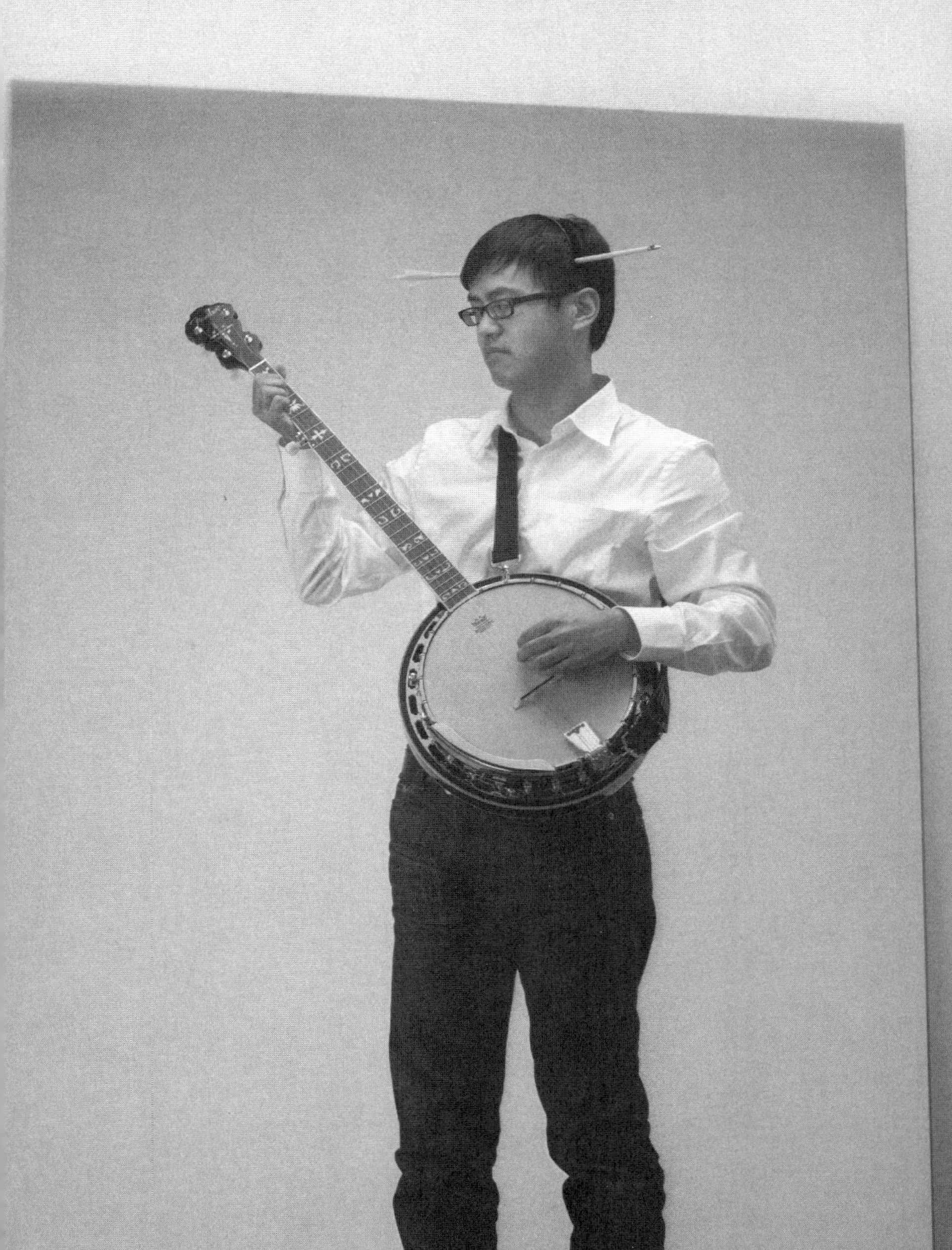

banjo and has even played with the world-renowned bluegrass musician Earl Scruggs. On *Let's Get Small* he says, now famously, "You just can't play a depressing song on the banjo." Lee had no previous experience with the instrument but decided to test this hypothesis by learning to play on it, over the course of his residency, one song. He selected Young's seminal guitar piece "My My, Hey Hey," which can be either melancholic or aggressive depending on whether it is played acoustically, as in the first track on *Rust Never Sleeps,* or electrically, as in the album's final track.

Lee's banjo version of "My My, Hey Hey" represents a third, bluegrass, version and is his first-ever audio piece. In a wry and comic move, he has installed *My My, Hey Hey (Out of the Blue) / Hey Hey, My My (Into the Black*), *Neil Young, 1979* (*Steve Martin, 1977*) (2007) in the Wattis Institute elevator, which carries visitors on a very short, one-story ride between the upper and lower floors, rather than in the gallery space allocated for his exhibition. The audio installation is almost anticlimactic, even reminiscent of Muzak, that often consumed but infrequently commented upon easy-listening filler found in malls, retail outlets, and nondescript transitional spaces. Ironically, as visitors think they are on their way to the "real" artworks, they experience the focal point of Lee's project. In another sideways move, the artist gives his banjo recording sculptural form as a limited-edition 12-inch vinyl record with his texts as the liner notes (this piece is on display in the foyer).

Lee conceived the two works that actually appear in the galleries (officially these are part of his solo *Passengers* exhibition as opposed to his Capp Street Project residency) as footnotes to the elevator piece. The single-channel video titled *Let's Get Small, Steve Martin, 1977* (2007) focuses on the opening of Martin's first live album and what was to become the comedian's tagline. Martin starts his routine by saying, "I'm sorry, I'm really pissed off." He criticizes the sound man, the audience, and the local population, accusing them of insulting him as a comedian. He becomes increasingly angry until he says, now famously, "Excuuuuse me." This catchphrase became a staple for him, his trademark, and inevitably the object of parody later on. Lee believes that Martin ultimately abandoned stand-up because everyone expected him to repeat this line, which was no longer funny *because* it was expected. For his piece, Lee reformats this moment by elongating the *u* in "Excuuuuse me" to last several minutes, creating the illusion of absurdly sustained anger. This mimicry through continual looping, the artificial building of frustration and exaggerated emotion, alludes to the entrapment of the comedian within what was once his own unique brand of humor.

My My, Hey Hey (Out of the Blue), Neil Young, 1979 and *Hey Hey, My My (Into the Black), Neil Young, 1979* (both 2007) are two photographs showing Lee's shadow in poses that he imagines Young might have adopted during the original *Rust Never Sleeps* concert. Lee holds an acoustic guitar in one picture, and an electric guitar in the other. The

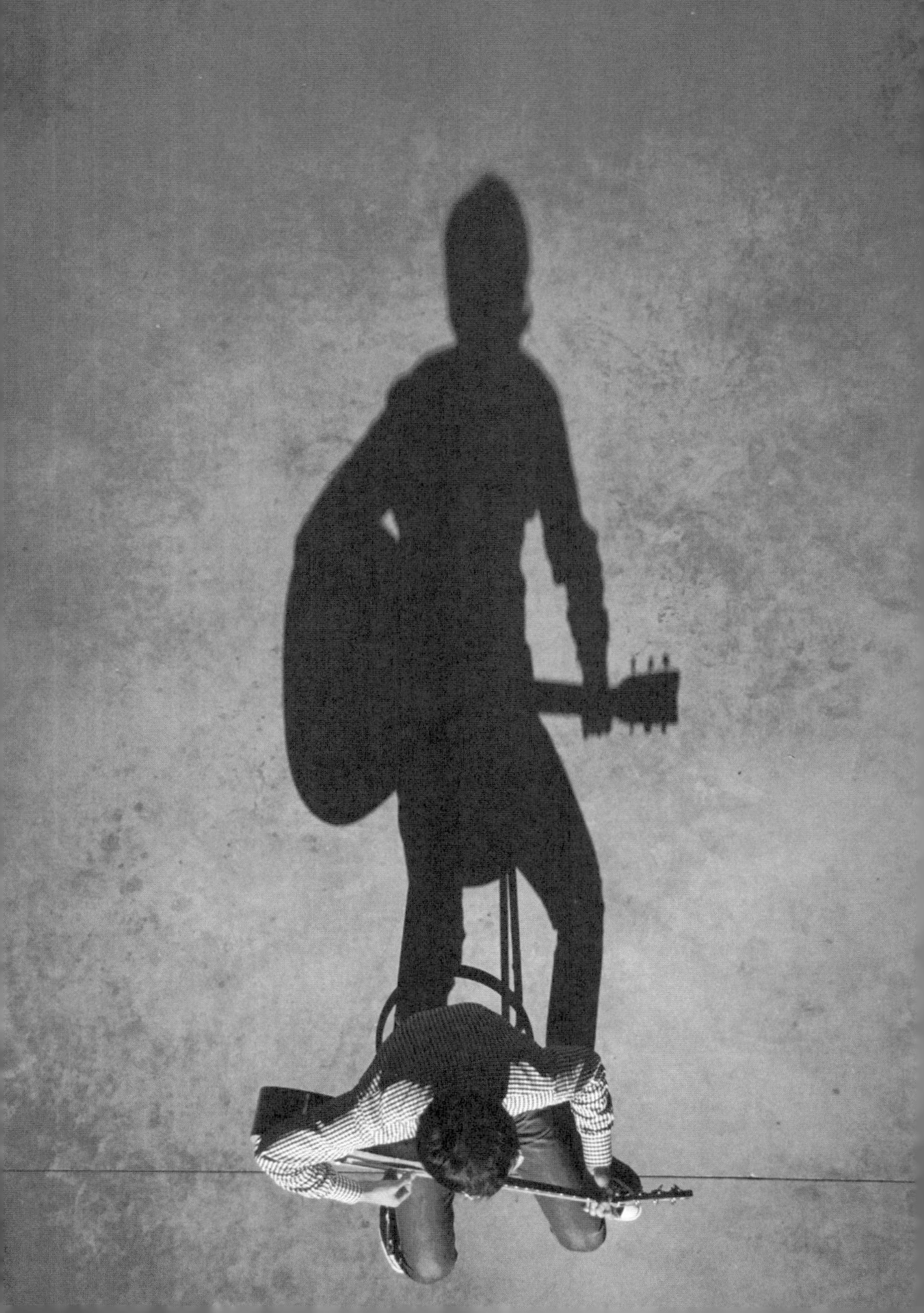

images materialize something intangible, capturing not an actual performance but some part of its remnants. This idea is integral to Lee's understanding of Young's creative output—that it is restless and undefined, and that both the musician's persona and his music have changed with each new album.

My My, Hey Hey (Out of the Blue), Neil Young, 1979, 2007
Chromogenic print
88 x 64 in. (223.5 x 162.6 cm)

Though the video and photographs treat Young and Martin separately, they form a triptych with the audio installation in the elevator. Collectively they become self-reflexive, mutually supporting, and they conflate the two artistic personae into an idiosyncratic, total history that represents in microcosm concerns that run throughout Lee's entire oeuvre. Lee referenced George and Ira Gershwin in *Funny Face,*

George & Ira Gershwin, 1927 (2002), the baseball player Ted Williams in *Untitled*

(Ted Williams, 1941) (2003), and the rap group Public Enemy in *It Takes a Nation of Millions to Hold Us Back, Public Enemy, 1988* (2006). Through each persona Lee speaks of creative origins: why an artist makes a particular work, and the historical moment and social conditions at the time of its making. Whether he is re-creating Iggy Pop's backflip in the ludicrous *Untitled (James Osterberg, 1970)* (2004) or roped to a chair hanging upside down in homage to Harry Houdini (although the photograph of his performance is hung upside down so it looks the right way up) in *Upside Down Water Torture Chamber, Harry Houdini, 1914* (2004), by taking on a variety of eccentric postures Lee also borrows their

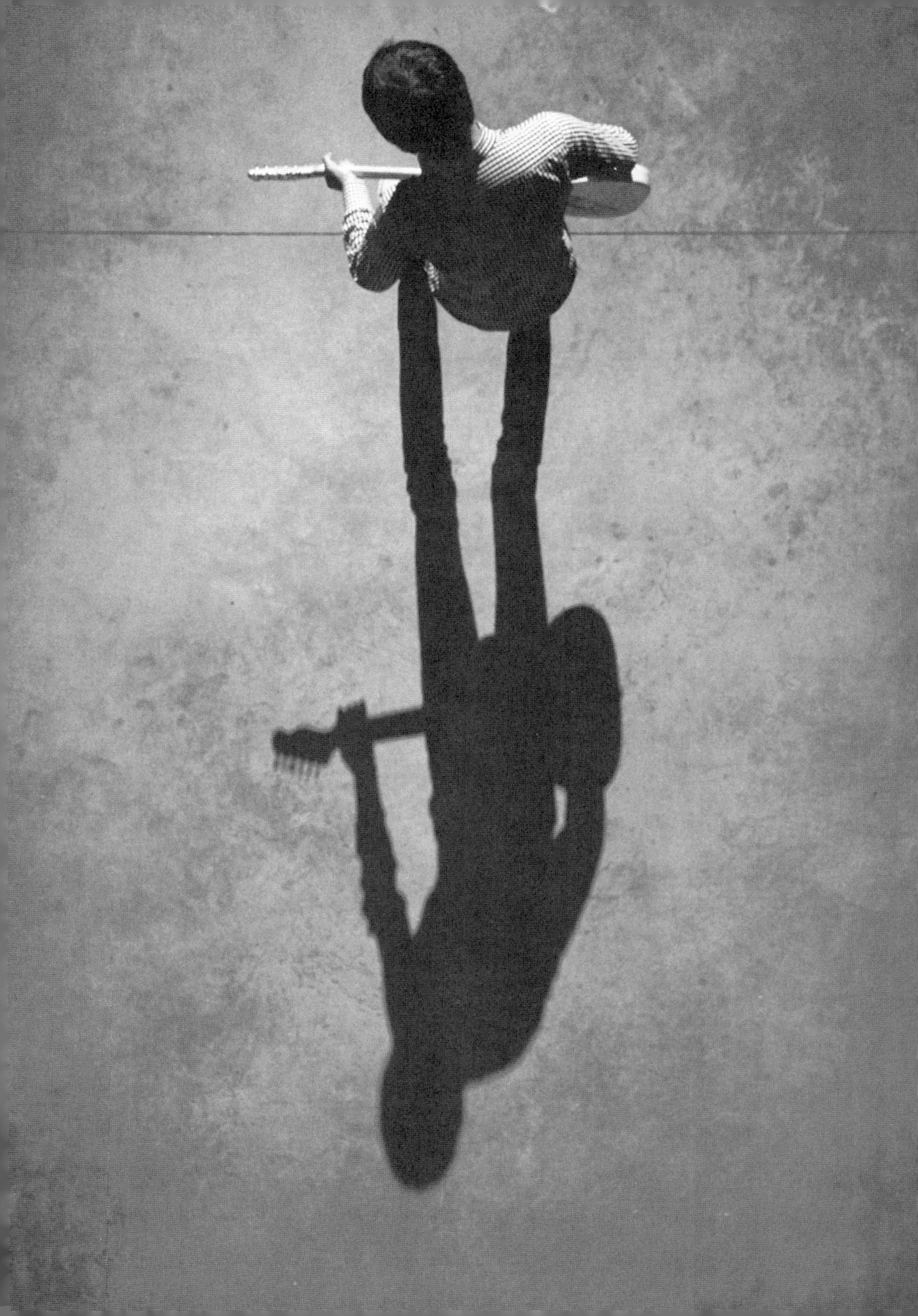

accompanying contexts. Although his characters are autonomous individuals, for the artist they exist within broader systems of representation, such as the genres from which they originate—for instance classical music, baseball, magic, comedy (as in Martin's case), or rock music (as in Young's)—and therefore connect to the landscapes, social histories, and politics of their places and times. In bringing together different characters and eras and manipulating them through formal strategies such as flipping, spinning, and role playing, Lee creates a language that is unique but has universal applications. He suggests that no one is fully segregated—that thinking about Johann Sebastian Bach in 1741, for example, might tell us something about Public Enemy in 1988, and maybe even Tim Lee in 2008.

Each of these figures also represents Lee's concept of the moment of the "proper name": the point at which a name comes to reference a single person rather than any of the other people who might share that name. Despite all the many Steve Martins in the world, the name *Steve Martin*, in the public imagination, refers to a single Steve Martin, and *Let's Get Small*, Lee suggests, is when it happened. Furthermore, Lee's idea of the proper name applies not just to the instant in which a public persona crystallizes, but also more broadly to the potential of such a public persona to shift. *Steve Martin* can actually refer to many different personae: the stand-up comedian of the 1970s, the family guy of his later comedy films, the art collector, or the contributor to the *New Yorker*. Neil Young's name is similarly iconic but can be associated with folk, electrified rock, country, electronica, swing, and grunge, and outside the realm of music with film direction, education, and social protest. Every one of his albums has been, Lee claims, a reaction to the one that preceded it. Lee's Capp Street Project looks at 1977–79 as a pivotal moment coincidentally shared, and also at how our ideas of Martin and Young have changed in the decades since.

Although Lee's pieces are performative, his role playing and associations are political rather than personal, particularly with respect to ideas of national identity and race. Neil Young is often thought to be American, although he was born in Canada and is still a Canadian citizen, and Lee believes that the musician's infatuation with America is actually part of his assertion of his Canadian identity. Lee, who was born in Seoul and now lives in Vancouver, references Young by examining the question of national identity through his own situation as a Korean Canadian in San Francisco. His evocation of Steve Martin makes the issue of race even more explicit. An important element of Martin's comedy in the 1970s was his play on his appearance as a Waspish male. When Lee performs as Martin, the fact that Lee is Asian is strikingly obvious, thereby calling even more attention to ethnicity than Martin did.

At the core of Lee's practice is a concern with the issues of particular figures at certain moments in their histories (and our larger cultural history). He takes on their problems and tries, in a sense, to resolve them while inevitably creating new problems for himself. These relationships are not about mimicry, but rather about transformation. Treating them as reference points, Lee attempts to articulate his own position, which is particularly interesting in the context of Neil Young and Steve Martin. In his research for this residency project Lee explored the various ways in which the musician and the comedian struggled with the public's expectations of their creativity—how Young's constant transformations have surprised, and sometimes confounded, his audience, and how Martin became trapped in his first persona and had to transform himself to reassert his creative freedom.

Lee, who may or may not have yet articulated his own "proper name," is in a special

fix: Does he play into or against expectations of his work? Are the problems of the
artist the same as those of the comedian or
the musician? Should Lee always be trying
to deliver something unexpected, unexpectedly? Can he hope, through his work,
to produce the equivalent of a catchphrase
or throw his audience for a loop? Is this
his moment of the proper name, or is it too
soon to tell?

TIM LEE

Born in Seoul, 1975
Lives and works in Vancouver

Solo Exhibitions

2008
Contemporary Arts Museum, Houston
(catalog)
Cohan and Leslie, New York
Johnen Galerie, Berlin
Capp Street Project: Tim Lee, CCA Wattis
Institute for Contemporary Arts,
San Francisco (catalog)
Passengers, CCA Wattis Institute for
Contemporary Arts, San Francisco
(brochure)

2007
Remakes, Variations (1741–2049), Presentation
House Gallery, North Vancouver, Canada
(catalog)
Galerie Rüdiger Schöttle, Munich

2006
Lisson Gallery, London
Cohan and Leslie, New York

2005
Tracey Lawrence Gallery, Vancouver

2004
Cohan and Leslie, New York
Tracey Lawrence Gallery, Vancouver

2003
Sight Gags, YYZ Artists' Outlet, Toronto

2002
Louie Louie, Or Gallery, Vancouver

2001
The Move, Western Front, Vancouver

Group Exhibitions

2008
Revolutions: Forms That Turn, Sydney Biennale
(catalog)
eXponential Future, Morris and Helen Belkin
Art Gallery, Vancouver (catalog)

2007
*All About Laughter: Humor in Contemporary
Art*, Mori Art Museum, Tokyo (catalog)
Acting the Part: Photography as Theatre,
Vancouver Art Gallery (catalog)
FOR SALE, Cristina Guerra, Lisbon (catalog)
Passengers, CCA Wattis Institute for
Contemporary Arts, San Francisco

2006
Wrong, Klosterfelde, Berlin
*Sliding Doors: Recent Contemporary
Acquisitions*, Tate Modern, London
El equilibrio y sus derivados, Casa del Lago,
Mexico City
Distor, Museo de Arte Carrillo Gil, Mexico City
Sound and Vision, Musée des beaux-arts,
Montreal
Portrait of a Citizen, Vancouver Art Gallery
Make Believe, Art Gallery of Alberta,
Edmonton, Canada

2005
New Work / New Acquisitions, Museum of
Modern Art, New York
Intertidal: Vancouver Art and Artists, Museum
van Hedendaagse Kunst Antwerpen,
Belgium (catalog)
L'envers des apparences, Musée d'art
contemporain, Montreal (catalog)
I Really Should . . ., Lisson Gallery, London
Belonging, Sharjah Biennial, United Arab
Emirates (catalog)

2004

*Anxiety of Influence: Bachelors, Brides, and
    a Family Romance*, Stadtgalerie Bern,
    Switzerland
Artists' Favourites, Institute of Contemporary
    Arts, London (catalog)
Perform, Tracey Lawrence Gallery, Vancouver
Confidence, Passagen, Linköpings Konsthall,
    Sweden
Building the Collection, Art Gallery of Ontario,
    Toronto
Game Over, Galerie SAW Gallery, Ottawa,
    Canada

2003

*Baja to Vancouver: The West Coast and Contem-
    porary Art*, Seattle Art Museum (traveled
    to the Museum of Contemporary Art San
    Diego; Vancouver Art Gallery; and the CCA
    Wattis Institute for Contemporary Arts, San
    Francisco) (catalog)
Video Heroes, Saidye Bronfman Centre for the
    Arts, Montreal (traveled to Cambridge
    Galleries, Canada)
Peripheries Become the Center, First Prague
    Biennial (catalog)
Soundtracks: Re-Play, Edmonton Art Gallery,
    Canada (traveled to Blackwood Gallery,
    Toronto; MacKenzie Art Gallery, Regina,
    Canada; and Ottawa Art Gallery, Canada)

2002

Vancouver Video, Nuova Icona, Venice
    (traveled to Folly Gallery, Lancaster,
    England) (catalog)
Binocular Parallax, Consolidated Works,
    Seattle
Dogwood, Morris and Helen Belkin Art Gallery,
    Vancouver (catalog)
Suite, Belkin Satellite, Vancouver

2001

Documents, Para/Site Art Space, Hong Kong

Selected Bibliography

Burnham, Clint. "Tim Lee." *Flash Art,* no. 240 (January–February 2005): 119.

Chasin, Noah. "Tim Lee." *Art Review* 2, no. 7 (June–August 2004): 94.

DeVuono, Frances. "Baja to Vancouver." *Artweek* 34, no. 10 (December 2003–January 2004): 13, 28.

———. "'Binocular Parallax' at Consolidated Works." *Artweek* 33, no. 10 (December 2002–January 2003): 27.

Helfand, Glen. "Baja to Vancouver." *Artforum* 42, no. 4 (December 2003): 150.

Henderson, Lee. "Lee's Way: The Comic Art of Tim Lee." *Border Crossings* 25, no. 3 (August 2006): 72–78.

Hoffmann, Jens, ed. *The Next Documenta Should Be Curated By An Artist.* Frankfurt am Main: Revolver Press, 2003.

———. "Tim Lee," in *Ice Cream: Contemporary Art in Culture.* London: Phaidon Press Limited, 2007.

———. "Tim Lee," in *Vitamin Ph: New Perspectives in Photography.* London: Phaidon Press Limited, 2006.

———. "When the Serious Is Tinted with Humour, It Makes a Nicer Colour," in *Spur04.* Frankfurt am Main: Revolver Press, 2004.

Hoffmann, Jens, and Joan Jonas. *Art Works: Perform.* London: Thames & Hudson, 2005.

Hoffman, Jens, and Ken Lum. "Tim Lee," in *Prague Biennale 1: Peripheries Become the Center.* Milan: Giancarlo Politi Editore, 2003.

Jahn, Jeff. "Baja to Vancouver." *Modern Painters* 16, no. 4 (winter 2003): 130, 132.

Kamps, Toby. "Tim Lee," in *Baja to Vancouver: The West Coast in Contemporary Art.* San Francisco: CCA Wattis Institute for Contemporary Arts, 2003.

O'Brien, Melanie. *d'Or.* Vancouver: Or Gallery, 2003.

Roelstraete, Dieter, and Scott Watson, eds. *Intertidal: Vancouver Art and Artists.* Antwerp, Belgium: Museum van Hedendaagse Kunst Antwerpen, 2005.

Shier, Reid, ed. *Tim Lee: Remakes, Variations (1741–2049).* North Vancouver: Presentation House Gallery; Zurich: JRP-Ringier, 2007.

Wilson, Michael. "Tim Lee." *Artforum* 44, no. 10 (summer 2006): 349.

Capp Street Project: Tim Lee
Exhibition: January 8, 2008–January 10, 2009
Residency: August 1–December 1, 2007
Organized by the CCA Wattis Institute for Contemporary Arts and curated
by Jens Hoffmann and Claire Fitzsimmons

Director: Jens Hoffmann
Deputy director: Claire Fitzsimmons
Assistant curator: Stacen Berg
Administrative coordinator: Sue Ellen Stone
Gallery manager: David Martin
Director of public relations: Brenda Tucker

Lead sponsorship for *Capp Street Project: Tim Lee* is provided by the Nimoy Foundation.

Founding support for CCA Wattis Institute for Contemporary Arts programs has been provided
by Phyllis C. Wattis and Judy and Bill Timken. Generous support provided by the Phyllis C. Wattis
Foundation, Grants for the Arts / San Francisco Hotel Tax Fund, Ann Hatch and Paul Discoe, and
the CCA Curator's Forum.

Thanks to Tim for his enthusiasm and meticulous attention to detail throughout the project.

Thanks to those at CCA who have contributed to this exhibition and publication: Susan Avila,
Stephen Beal, Chris Bliss, Kathy Butler, Brian Conley, Patricia Flores, Sarrita Hunn, John Jenkins,
Barbara Jones, David Kirschman, Erin Lampe, Jen McKay, Kate Moore, Jim Norrena, Larry Rinder,
Aaron Spafford, Ingrid Steber, Ken Tanzer, Brenda Tucker, Luke Turner, Michael Welch, and
Lindsey Westbrook.

Additional thanks to Katharine DeShaw, Nicholas Logsdail, Jessica Morgan, Kitty Scott, and
Jon Sueda.

Many thanks to Johnen + Schöttle, Cologne/Berlin; Lisson Gallery, London; and Cohan and Leslie,
New York for their kind support of this exhibition and publication.

Special thanks to Ann Hatch, chair of CCA's Board of Trustees and founder of Capp Street Project.

The artist would like to thank Stacen Berg, Joseph del Pesco, Claire Fitzsimmons, Jens Hoffmann,
Uke Lorenz, Job Piston, Ian Reeves, Sue Ellen Stone, Andrew Tosiello, and the CCA Wattis Institute.

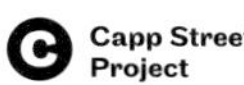

Founded in San Francisco in 1983, Capp Street Project was the first visual arts residency program
in the United States dedicated solely to the creation and presentation of new art installations.
Since its inception, Capp Street Project has given more than 100 local, national, and international
artists the opportunity to create new work. It became part of the CCA Wattis Institute in 1998.

This publication accompanies *Capp Street Project: Tim Lee* at the CCA Wattis Institute for Contemporary Arts, on view January 8, 2008–January 10, 2009, in the Logan Galleries on the San Francisco campus of California College of the Arts.

Editors: Jens Hoffmann and Claire Fitzsimmons
Authors: Claire Fitzsimmons, Jens Hoffmann, and Tim Lee
Catalog design: Stripe / Jon Sueda
Copy editor: Lindsey Westbrook
Director of publications: Erin Lampe
Printer: Creative Litho, Foster City, California
Print brokerage: Celeste McMullin, The Printcess

ISBN: 978-0-9802055-0-3

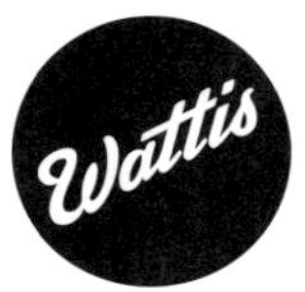

**CCA Wattis Institute
for Contemporary Arts**
Kent and Vicki Logan Galleries
1111 Eighth Street
San Francisco CA 94107
415.551.9210 / www.wattis.org

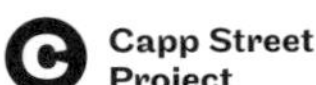

**Capp Street
Project**